WASHTENAW COUNTY BIKE RIDES

"It is no exaggeration to affirm that a journey by bicycle is like none other; it is a thing apart; it has a tempo and a style of its own."

. . .

"Any touring bicyclist can relate the feeling of carefree abandon and catharsis that pedaling evokes as layers upon layers of mental and emotional encrustations are shed. Each turn, each hill is another discovery illuminating a place, a sensation and a perception until then hidden from view. Nothing is so utterly alive and well as the spirit of the touring bicyclist."

James E. Starrs, *The Noiseless Tenor*

WASHTENAW COUNTY BIKE RIDES

A GUIDE TO ROAD RIDES IN AND AROUND ANN ARBOR

Joel D. Howell

The University of Michigan Press • Ann Arbor

Copyright © by the University of Michigan 2009
All rights reserved
Published in the United States of America by
The University of Michigan Press
Manufactured in the United States of America
∞ Printed on acid-free paper

2012   2011   2010   2009   4   3   2   1

A CIP catalog record for this book is available from the British Library.

Library of Congress Cataloging-in-Publication Data

Howell, Joel D.
   Washtenaw County bike rides : A guide to road rides in and
around Ann Arbor / Joel D. Howell.
      p.   cm.
   Includes bibliographical references.
   ISBN-13: 978-0-472-03330-0 (pbk. : alk. paper)
   ISBN-10: 0-472-03330-1 (pbk. : alk. paper)
   1. Bicycle touring—Michigan—Washtenaw County—Guidebooks.
2. Washtenaw County (Mich.)—Guidebooks. I. Title.

GV1045.5.M52W374   2009
796.5109774'35—dc22   2008038945

Royalties from the sale of this book will be donated to the
Lucien W. Chaney Bicycling Safety & Advocacy Fund.

To Linda,

my partner on bike rides

and in life.

ACKNOWLEDGMENTS

I offer thanks to Dan Harrison, Robert Paine, and Linda Samuelson for careful review of the manuscript, the Ann Arbor District Library for its excellent resources on Washtenaw County history and geography, and the Ann Arbor Bicycle Touring Society for inspiring me to explore the byways of Washtenaw County. I also thank Jim DuFresne for his excellent work on the maps in this book.

CONTENTS

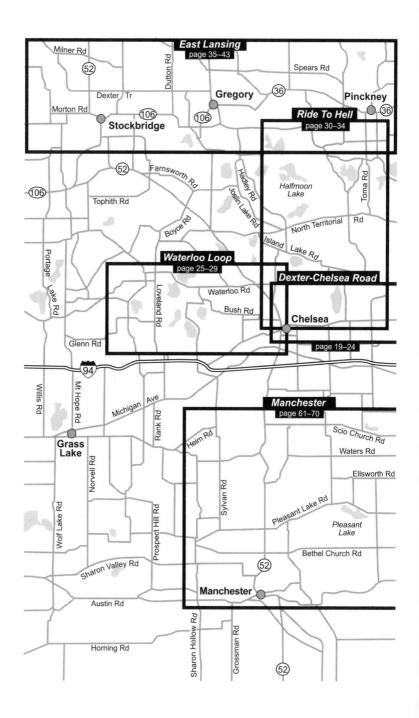

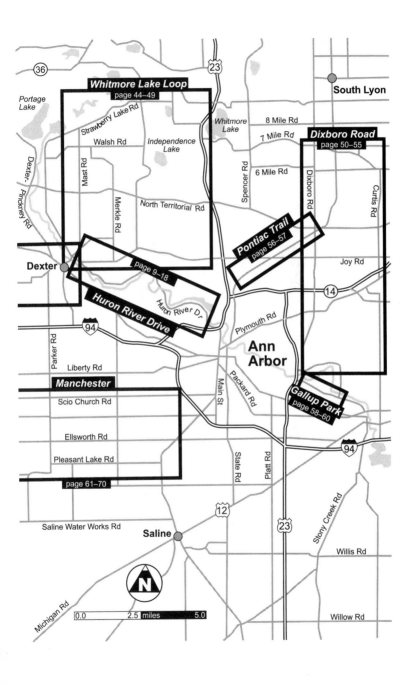

Legend

The maps in this book use the following symbols. Mileage flags mark distances along the route.

1.5 mi	Mileage flag
	Direction of travel
	Parking area
	Park or natural area
	Railroad tracks
	Trail or bike path
Ride to Hell page 31	Adjacent ride, link, or route option

RIDING TIPS

*I*nterspersed throughout the book are topical sections offering helpful hints on practical issues in road riding. These suggestions may help you ride more enjoyably and safely as you face the inevitable but often unexpected challenges that road riders must deal with from time to time.

> *"It is by riding a bicycle that you learn the contours of a country best, since you have to sweat up the hills and can coast down them. Thus you remember them as they actually are . . . you have no such accurate remembrance of a country you have driven through as you gain by riding a bicycle."*
>
> Ernest Hemingway, in *By-Line*

INTRODUCTION

This book is a guide for people who want to go bike riding on the roads of Washtenaw County. It's for people who are new to the county, perhaps moving there to attend college or take up a new job. It's for people who are new to bike riding and want some suggestions about where they can ride. It is also for more experienced bicyclists who want to expand their repertoire of rides or learn a bit more about where they are riding.

All the routes described in this book start or end in Washtenaw County, Michigan, although some edge into neighboring counties. There are many potential routes. The criterion for selecting the rides is simply that each route is one I like and have ridden many times. The routes are also selected with a strong preference for rides outside of cities.

Washtenaw County has an active city life but has retained (at least for now) both woods and farms, which makes for a wide range of pleasant bike rides. The dominant city is Ann Arbor, home to the University of Michigan, but the county has a diverse range of communities and environments. There are lots of pleasant towns and villages throughout the county, many of which are visited on the rides described here. The rides in this book go predominantly north and west of Ann Arbor into the less-populated regions of the county. Rides to the north tend to be somewhat more wooded and perhaps a bit hillier; those to the south feature more open space and, when the winds blow, less shelter from the wind and a greater chance of a windy ride.

All of these rides can be done on a road bike—the sort of narrow-tire bike that many members of the baby boom generation know as a "ten speed" (though most today offer more than 10 speeds). However,

A bicyclist on Huron River Drive heading out of Ann Arbor

all of these rides can also be done on any sort of bicycle; a hybrid (cross bike) or mountain bike will work fine. The only issue is whether you feel comfortable riding long distances on something other than a road bike—and that judgment will vary for each rider.

All of these routes are paved. Thus, routes specific to mountain biking are not included. There is excellent mountain biking available in the area, but that's not the subject of this book. Riders on a mountain or cross bike can easily go down dirt roads, and many of the rides in the book connect with dirt roads that make for wonderful riding. Those who like that sort of riding are encouraged to explore these options, which are occasionally noted but not detailed.

HOW TO USE THIS BOOK

The book's intent is to provide the rider with the sort of flexibility necessary to produce the ideal ride for a given rider on a given day with a given group or by oneself. The routes provide a set of options from which to select, combine, or mix and match.

The reasons for this flexibility are at least threefold. For one thing, it's hard to calibrate rides across a wide range of riders. One person's "killer" hill is another person's barely perceptible rise. One person's "long" ride is a warm-up for another. One person hates riding anywhere close to cars while another is quite comfortable with heavy traffic. People differ. This book attempts to offer all sorts of riders some enjoyable rides.

Second, each day is different. Do you want a hard ride or an easier one? Do you want a short ride or an all-day one? Located on the western edge of the Eastern Time Zone, summertime offers Washtenaw County riders the chance to ride relatively late into the evening, with some sunsets in June and July occurring well after 9:00 p.m. Washtenaw County also offers the opportunity to enjoy all four seasons of the year, and while year-round bicycle riding poses challenges it also offers rewards.

Finally, at the outset of a ride it's not always possible to predict how it will go. Some days you will find that you feel strong while on other days you may want to relax. Sometimes the weather cooperates, sometimes not so much. The point of this book is to provide you with

Snowy trees frame Huron River Drive on a wintry day

In the southern part of the county the scenery features fewer forests and more open fields

a range of options. You can use those options to decide what you want to do on a given day, including the option of changing in the midst of a ride. That way you can enjoy some of the variety that the area has to offer while creating a ride that is just the one you want.

THE RIDES

Each ride starts with the route's length. This is followed by "links," other named routes in this book with which the route can link. There are also "options," alternative routes or extensions from the given route that may or may not link up with another ride.

Many riders will be able to ride their bikes to the starting point. For those who will be driving, there are parking suggestions, but please take care to honor any parking restrictions or limits that may be in place!

The route is given twice. First, there is a description of what to expect on that ride as well as information about its sights, sounds, and smells. Following that description is a cue sheet for those who just want to know where to go and where to turn. All distances are in miles. Compass directions are approximate.

The essence of this arrangement is the ability to mix and match routes, to use the links and options to combine rides or discover something new. You can go out on one route and come back on another. You can combine two short routes to make a longer one or combine two long routes for a full day in the saddle!

Although the routes are described as proceeding in one direction, do not forget that you can ride each one in the opposite direction for what is often a very different experience. *Be careful when following a route.* Things change. Road conditions change. Some roads with a great surface may deteriorate; some crumbling roads will be resurfaced. Some of these rides go over bridges that need repair. Roads may be impassable while repairs are ongoing. Changing road conditions are a fact of life, especially for bicycle riders seeking quiet roads that are less used by cars than the main thoroughfares. Caution is advised. Should you find any impassable obstacles, the routes listed will usually provide you a way of getting around them.

RIDE CATEGORIES

RIDES WITH CHILDREN ON TRAINING WHEELS OR WITH CHILDREN WHO ARE JUST LEARNING TO RIDE: Gallup Park, Hudson Mills Metropark (see the North Territorial Extension under the "Huron River Drive" ride).

RIDES OVER 45 MILES: East Lansing, Manchester.

RIDES WITH HILLS: Dixboro Road, Manchester, Ride to Hell, Joy Road (see the Joy Road Extension under the "Huron River Drive" ride). Riders who are seeking long hills will find none in Washtenaw County. A guide to shorter hills in the city of Ann Arbor can be found at the Ann Arbor Bicycle Touring Society Web site.

ESPECIALLY SCENIC RIDES: Huron River Drive, Waterloo Loop, Manchester.

AREA BIKE CLUBS AND OTHER USEFUL ORGANIZATIONS

One of the best ways to learn more about riding or routes is to join one of the local biking groups. Riding with a club is a good way to learn about the area rides and how to ride. It's a good way to get to know people who ride like you and find people with whom to ride (if that's what you like to do). It will also help you learn the local mores. Each group has a Web site that will serve as an entrée to much more information.

Ann Arbor Bicycle Touring Society (AABTS), www.aabts.org

This is the society with which I first rode in Washtenaw County. I am grateful to the AABTS for starting me and others on what has become a bicycle obsession. Riders of all ages, speeds, shapes, and proclivities are welcome and are well represented on club rides. The Web site provides links to the almost daily rides, and nonmembers may participate free of charge. Club members receive discounts at most local bicycle shops. Each July the club sponsors "One Helluva Ride" in which 1,500 to 2,000 participants enjoy road rides of 15 to 100 miles, as well as mountain bicycle rides. The Web site offers a wide range of maps and routes, some of which overlap the routes described in more detail in this book. For anyone wishing to learn more about routes throughout the county and beyond, this is the place to go.

Washtenaw Bicycling and Walking Coalition, www.wbwc.org

This local organization combines an interest in bicycling and walking. It pays particular attention to issues of bicycle commuting, especially for year-round commuters, as well as safety issues for pedestrians and bicyclists. The group's Web site is a treasure trove of news coverage and local governance related to bicycling.

Michigan Wolver-bents, www.lmb.org/wolverbents/index.htm

Do you ride a recumbent bicycle? Do you want to know about issues specific to recumbent bicycles? If so, this organization and its Web site are for you!

Ann Arbor Velo Club, www.aavc.org

The Ann Arbor Velo Club is a group of bicyclists interested in racing with the mission of developing skills and abilities across all groups (junior riders, senior men and women, and masters racers). The group fields several racing teams each year and has Michigan's largest racing club roster.

University of Michigan Cycling Team, www.mcycling.org/index.php

This team is open to any student at the University of Michigan regardless of skill or experience.

Washtenaw County Heritage Tours, www.ewashtenaw.org/ government/departments/planning_environment/historic_ preservation/histweb_tours/home.html

While it is not a bicycle organization per se, the Washtenaw County Heritage Map initiative has created four driving tours of Washtenaw County, which provide a wonderful guide to the area's architecture and history. Each tour comes with a brochure and detailed maps. The tours overlap some of the routes in this book and can easily be incorporated into a ride.

$\mathcal{H}$URON RIVER DRIVE

ROUTE: Ann Arbor (Wheeler Park) to Dexter, 10.1 miles

LINKS WITH: Dexter-Chelsea Road, Whitmore Lake Loop

OPTIONS: Alternative starts A and B
Joy Road Extension
Webster Church Road Extension
North Territorial Extension (links to East Lansing
Route and Ride to Hell)

PARKING: Street parking near Wheeler Park, Ann Arbor. Note
that there is sometimes a time limit on street parking.
See alternative start A for other parking options. There
is street parking available in Dexter. You can also park a
vehicle at any of the parks passed on the route.

*This winding road along the Huron River is perhaps the favorite
bicycle ride out of Ann Arbor, featuring almost ten miles of riding
without even a stop sign.*

One of the standard ways for bicyclists to ride out of Ann Arbor, this
lovely road along the Huron River can nicely serve as the jumping-off
point for many of the longer rides described in this book. Huron River
Drive is an immensely popular route; on a pleasant summer morning
the bikes on the road can easily outnumber the cars. As a result, people
who drive this road regularly are accustomed to seeing bicycles. In
addition, the speed limit is 35, there are lots of "share the road" signs
to alert drivers to the fact that this is a widely used bike route, runners
are another common sight, and the winding road keeps cars moving
slower than they might otherwise. Thus, for beginning riders (such
as children) this is a good first road ride out of town as long as the

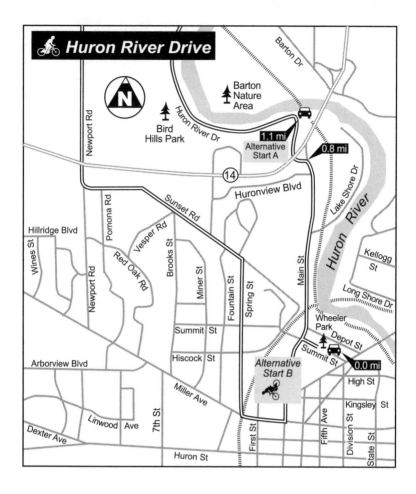

rider is comfortable maintaining the bike in a straight line. Caution is always in order when sharing the road.

Start in Ann Arbor at Wheeler Park, located between Fourth and Fifth Avenue and Depot and Summit Streets, where parking is available on the surrounding streets. This is the starting point for many Ann Arbor Bicycle Touring Society club rides, including the weekly ride to Dexter and points west.

ALTERNATIVE START A. A couple of convenient gravel parking lots are located near the start of the ride on the north side of Huron River Drive. One is located at the foot of the hill that starts the drive; another is a mile down the road. They are located at either end of the Barton Nature Area, an Ann Arbor

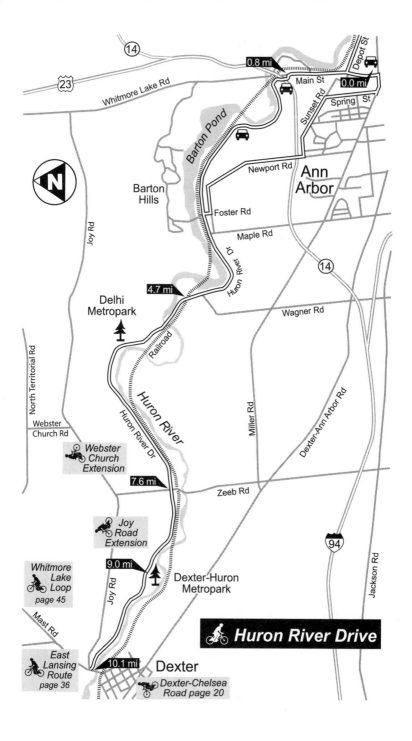

14

23

Whitmore Lake Rd

0.8 mi

Main St

Depot St

0.0 mi

Sunset Rd

Spring St

Barton Pond

Newport Rd

Ann Arbor

N

Barton Hills

Foster Rd

Maple Rd

Huron River Dr

14

Joy Rd

4.7 mi

Delhi Metropark

Wagner Rd

Railroad

Huron River

Miller Rd

Dexter-Ann Arbor Rd

North Territorial Rd

Webster Church Rd

Webster Church Extension

Huron River Dr

7.6 mi

Zeeb Rd

Joy Road Extension

94

Whitmore Lake Loop page 45

9.0 mi

Dexter-Huron Metropark

Jackson Rd

Mast Rd

Joy Rd

East Lansing Route page 36

10.1 mi

Dexter

🚴 **Huron River Drive**

Dexter-Chelsea Road page 20

Park. Starting the bike ride at one of these places can be especially useful for rides with children or for those who do not want to ride their bicycles through town.

ALTERNATIVE START B.   An alternative bicycle route to Huron River Drive from Wheeler Park can be taken by going up and around on Newport Road. Instead of turning right on Main Street, turn left (south) on Main and then right (east) on Miller Avenue. After you come down a short hill and under a railroad viaduct, turn right (north) on Spring Street. This takes you up some nice hills to Sunset Road. Turn left (west) on Sunset, then right (north) on Newport. The road descends, losing all the altitude gained so far. You will pass over an expressway (M-14) and past Bird Road, a turnoff to Bird Hills Park. (If you want to do more than one loop around the hills of Spring and Sunset and you don't mind a short stretch of gravel road, you can turn onto Bird Road, take it to Huron River Drive, take Huron River Drive back to Main Street, take Main to Miller Avenue, and repeat the process.) Newport eventually turns to the left (west), and you can then turn right (north) onto a short stretch of Foster Road or Maple Road to get to Huron River Drive, where you will turn left (west). This will add only about 0.3 miles to the basic route.   ❖

For the main route, leave the park and turn left (west) on Summit Street. At 0.1 miles turn right (north) onto Main Street. The ride up Main can be busy. Turn left (west) at 0.8 miles onto Huron River Drive, a turn that requires close attention. You will need to make a left turn immediately before the road enters the expressway (M-14). If traffic is heavy, you may wish to pull off to the right and wait for a break in the flow. You will encounter a stop sign and then will cross a curving road with limited vision for both you and the oncoming drivers. Drivers who have just exited the expressway will be traveling at a high rate of speed and might not have bicycles on their minds. Be careful. However, the only major difficulty arises on football Saturdays, when tens of thousands of people arrive to witness the Maize and Blue confront its opponent du jour. Many people will be exiting the expressway on this road, and it might take a long time to cross the line of traffic. Thus, it is a good idea to time your ride so as to avoid crossing Main Street within two or three hours of game time or to use one of the alternative starts.

Cross the road and enter Huron River Drive. Roll down the hill and settle in—you'll have not so much as a stop sign for the next ten miles! The first gravel parking lot for alternative start A is located on the right at the bottom of the hill, mile 1.1. The next mile takes you through a tunnel of thick, overhanging trees, which nicely frame

The Huron River makes for a pleasant companion as this bicyclist heads east on Huron River drive back toward Ann Arbor.

glimpses of the river in spring and summer. Come winter, with the leaves off the trees (Michigan is a four-season state!), you will enjoy excellent river views here and all along the route. You also—at the time of this writing—will have some rough pavement to contend with, but road improvements are in the works.

At mile 2.0 the views of the road open up and you come to the second gravel parking lot described in alternative start A on the right-hand side of the road. For the next couple of miles you have houses on the left and river views on the right, including some nice vistas across the river to the village of Barton Hills. Alternative start B joins the road at mile 3.3. To the right, Foster Road can take you over a bridge and, after a short stretch of tightly packed dirt road, into the community of Barton Hills. Barton Hills has, not surprisingly, some hills, which are short but very steep. You can link through Barton Hills to Whitmore Lake Road and the Whitmore Lake Loop.

At mile 3.6 you start a long, horseshoe curve that follows the river on the right; this is my favorite scenery of the entire ride. Be careful crossing the railroad tracks at mile 4.7. Soon there begins a gradual climb to the top of a hill at mile 5.3, followed by the steepest downhill of the route (which will be, as is usually the case, the steepest uphill on the return!). Near the bottom of this hill on your left is Delhi

Metropark. If you want to, stop at the park and enjoy a rest by the river. On busy days you can zip past the cars lined up to pay admission and get in free—you're on a bike! The park has water and toilets. It also has a canoe livery if you are in the mood for a multisport outing.

While at (or riding past) Delhi Metropark and catching glimpses of the Huron River to your left, it is interesting to consider the thriving communities that once dotted the river's shores. The Huron River drops about 8 feet per mile, and thus represented an important and easily tapped power source during the nineteenth century. In the latter half of the century this area was the site of a thriving industrial village with a several mills (one rising to four stories), its own post office, and a railroad station that saw four railroad stops a day. It was named Delhi in 1846 after the area's dells and hills. But by the end of the century steam power was quickly replacing water power. The mills were closed by 1903, and a tornado in 1917 administered the coup de grâce to this once promising village. It's hard to imagine the current site as an industrial complex, but you can still see traces of the old mills alongside the bridge.

Once you've had your fill of Delhi Metropark, continue up the road. Enjoy the gentle curves and hills with the Huron River on your left, remaining aware of traffic from the (ever increasing) housing developments on your right. At mile 7.6 you come to Zeeb Road. This, too, was once the site of a mill complex and the associated community known as Scio, which was founded in 1831. Here, like Delhi, there was a sawmill, flour mill, and feed mill, a post office, and regular train service. Millard Fillmore, who was to become the thirteenth U.S. president, purchased land here and visited several times. But by the early twentieth century this village, too, had seen its time in the industrial sun come to an end, and little of the original complex is visible today.

The corner of Zeeb Road and Huron River Drive is also the turning point for the optional Joy Road and Webster Church Road Extensions, which share the first section up to Joy Road.

- **OPTIONAL JOY ROAD EXTENSION** (alternative to the end of the Huron River Drive route, additional 0.4 miles). This is a good extension if you want to add a few decent hills but not much in the way of distance to the usual route. Turn right (north) on Zeeb Road and go up and over the gradual hill to the stop sign at Joy Road. Take a look at the field directly in front of you, where you will occasionally find whimsical sculptures made from rolls of hay—such as a black cat for Halloween. Turn left (west) and proceed down Joy Road, noting, perhaps, the centennial farm (a farm that has been in the same family for over one hundred years). After a gentle stretch that passes some farms, a few brief but steep hills will grab your attention. At the stop sign you are only a few yards north of the end of the Huron River Drive route.

- **OPTIONAL WEBSTER CHURCH ROAD EXTENSION** (a total of 8.8 miles out and back to the corner of Zeeb Road and Huron River Drive). This is a good extension if you want some variety from the usual route; you also get to pass by an interesting old church. Turn right (north) on Zeeb Road and go up and over the gradual hill to the stop sign at Joy Road. Take a look at

Haystacks become a friendly black cat around Halloween at the corner of Zeeb Road and Joy Road.

Webster Church on Webster Church Road, completed in 1835, is the oldest church in the county. The spire was taller before it was struck by lightning in 1914.

the field directly in front of you, where you will occasionally find whimsical sculptures made from rolls of hay—such as a black cat for Halloween. Then turn right (east) on Joy road (turning left will put you on the Joy Road Extension). After a mile the paved road turns left (north) and becomes Webster Church Road, a pleasant ride north with fields and forests on your way. (If you are on an appropriate bike, going straight on Joy Road leads to some peaceful dirt road riding.)

After another mile you will see the Webster United Church of Christ on your right. Completed in 1835 with donations from Daniel Webster, it's the oldest church in Washtenaw County, albeit with a shorter spire than it once had due to a 1914 lightning strike. In another 2.3 miles you come to North Territorial Road. The best option is to turn around and come back the same way, as the traffic on North Territorial means that this section of road cannot be recommended. On making the turn, look for blue heron nests high in the trees on your right. (If you have a cross bike or a mountain bike you can extend your route by continuing on Webster Church Road as it becomes a dirt road and enjoy a nice ride to Independence Lake County Park.) When you return to Zeeb Road you can turn left to go south to Huron River Drive, or go straight to take the Joy Road Extension. ❖

RIDING WITH (OR PAST) DOGS

Most dogs are not interested in bicycles and bicycle riders, and most dogs that are interested are unlikely to come chasing out into the road. But some are. Often simply yelling "No!" or "Stop!" will slow the dog down long enough for you to leave its territory, and most (though not all) will not chase you far beyond what they consider to be the boundary lines of their territories.

But some will. When that happens, one way to stop the dog is a squirt from a water bottle, but that requires that you have the bottle in your hand and you let the dog get close enough to squirt it in the face. If you do, this is an effective and harmless way to stop almost any chase. Simply getting off the bike might also work, as some dogs will stop once there is no longer the excitement of the chase.

A dog charging into the road at you can be a frightening experience. If you decide to stay on the bike, remember to keep riding. It's far too easy to get distracted and drift off into gravel on the side of the road or out into traffic, either of which can be far more dangerous than the dog. Ride the bike. Think about what you are going to do when a dog comes after you *before* it happens and you will be more likely to come away with a good story than an injury.

At mile 9.0 is Dexter-Huron Metropark, an excellent destination if you want to spend some time by the river catching your breath, going to the bathroom, getting some water, or, if you have carried a snack, grabbing a bite to eat. At mile 10.1 you reach the stop sign at Mast Road. There you can find food and drink at a convenience store at the confluence of Huron River Drive, Joy Road, and Mast Road. In the fall a delightful cider mill on the other side of the river, in operation since 1886, offers fresh cider and doughnuts in season and sometimes a few wasps as well! If you go into Dexter, which is less than a mile south, you will find a coffee shop and bakery.

Options from the end of this ride include the North Territorial Extension, the start of the Dexter-Chelsea Route, and the Whitmore Lake Loop.

- **OPTIONAL NORTH TERRITORIAL EXTENSION** (see map, p. 20), out and back ride, total of 6.0 miles, links to Ride to Hell and the East Lansing

Route. This is a convenient way to add a few miles to your ride by continuing another 3.0 miles on Huron River Drive. Cross Mast Road and continue on Huron River Drive. A few gently rolling hills will take you to North Territorial Road. North Territorial is busy, and extended travel on it is not recommended. You can, with care, go a short distance left (west) on North Territorial to reach the Hudson Mills Metropark. If you want to enter Hudson Mills through an alternative entrance, you can turn left into the park from Huron River Drive through a "back door" entrance at mile 12.9. The park's history harkens back to the days when water was a key source of power. This was the site in the mid-1800s of a sawmill and gristmill, known as Hudson Mill, as well as a general store, hotel, and pulp mill. Not much remains of the settlement, but you can still see the stone foundation of one of the mills inside the park.

Hudson Mills offers a nice 3.5 mile paved loop that is excellent for children learning to ride or people who want a relaxing spin without having to worry about cars. ❖

ROUTE CUES:

0.0   Start at Wheeler Park, Ann Arbor. Go west on Summit Street.
0.1   Turn right (north) on Main Street.
0.8   Turn left (west) on Huron River Drive.
4.7   Cross railroad tracks.
7.6   Cross Zeeb Road.
     Start of optional Joy Road Extension and Webster Church Road Extension.
10.1   Stop sign at Mast Road, Dexter.
     Start of optional North Territorial Extension.

RIDING WITH CARS: GENERAL PRINCIPLES

Road riding is, by definition, riding on the road, and most of the rides described in this book will have you sharing the pavement with cars. Cars are big, they move fast, and riding safely should always be on your mind. You will be safest if you ride with traffic and observe all of the traffic signs and signals, especially stoplights and stop signs. This is not only safer, but it helps to promote positive relationships with drivers, a good thing for all of us on bicycle wheels. Act like a car. Be courteous. Be predictable.

> *"The bicycle ran with a special ease at dusk, the tire
> emitting a kind of whisper as it palpated each rise and
> dip in the hard earth along the edge of the road."*
> Vladimir Nabokov, *Mary*

Dexter-Chelsea Road

ROUTE: Dexter to Chelsea, 8.2 miles

LINKS WITH: Huron River Drive
Whitmore Lake Loop
Waterloo Loop
Ride to Hell

OPTIONS: Downtown Dexter
Parker Road (links to Manchester)

PARKING: Street parking and free public parking lots can be
found in both Dexter and Chelsea.

*This is a mostly straight, mostly flat road between two Washtenaw
County villages; the route also serves as an entrée to western
Washtenaw County.*

Start at the end of Huron River Drive, the stop sign at Mast Road. At
the stop sign turn left (south, the road name changes to Central) to
pass over the Huron River and enter the village of Dexter. In the fall,
you may choose to stop at the old cider mill on the river at mile 0.2
for some cider and doughnuts. Wind your way through town, noting
the pleasant, tree-lined streets and old houses.

- **OPTIONAL DOWNTOWN DEXTER ROUTE.** Many shops are easily visible if
you want to head into the center of town to stop at a coffee shop, bakery,
or diner, or just to enjoy the Greek revival architecture. Simply go straight
on Central and turn right onto Main Street.   ❖

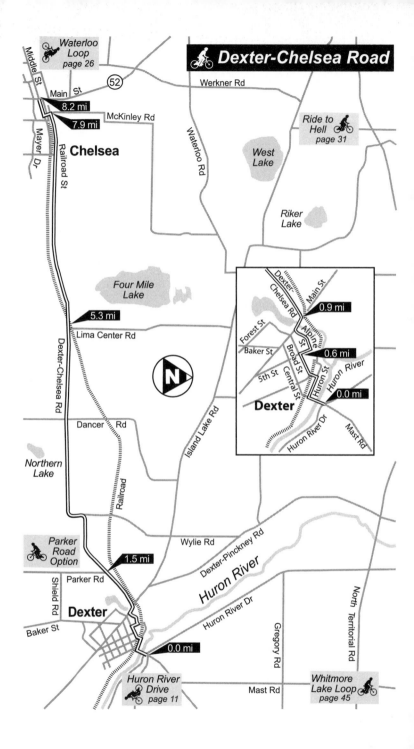

Waterloo
Loop
page 26

Middle St

Main St
8.2 mi

McKinley Rd
7.9 mi

Mayer Dr

Railroad St

Chelsea

Werkner Rd

Waterloo Rd

Ride to
Hell
page 31

West
Lake

Riker
Lake

Four Mile
Lake

5.3 mi

Lima Center Rd

Dexter-Chelsea Rd

Dexter-
Chelsea Rd

Main St

0.9 mi

Alpine St

Forest St

Baker St

Broad St

5th St

Central St

Huron St

0.6 mi

Huron River

Dexter

0.0 mi

Huron River Dr

Mast Rd

N

Dancer Rd

Railroad

Northern
Lake

Island Lake Rd

Parker
Road
Option

1.5 mi

Parker Rd

Shield Rd

Dexter

Baker St

Wylie Rd

Dexter-Pinckney Rd

Huron River

Huron River Dr

Gregory Rd

North Territorial Rd

0.0 mi

Huron River
Drive
page 11

Mast Rd

Whitmore
Lake Loop
page 45

A cider mill in Dexter offers you the chance to relax with fresh apple cider and more.

To bypass the village center and avoid some traffic, from Central turn right (west) onto Huron Street at mile 0.2, then left (south) at the next stop sign onto Broad Street, passing over the railroad tracks and by the Dexter train station on your right. These are the main tracks from Detroit to Chicago. They still carry passenger trains, but those trains no longer stop in Dexter.

Continue into Dexter and turn right (northwest) onto 5th Street shortly before reaching the center of town at mile 0.6. The road will turn left (south) and become Alpine Road. After passing the site of the farmer's market you will reach Main Street at mile 0.8. (If you want to visit the local shops, turn left here.) Taking care, as this can be a busy road, turn right (northwest) and then *immediately* turn left (southwest) *before* passing under the railroad overpass at mile 0.9.

This will put you on Dexter-Chelsea Road, and from here it's a pleasant, relatively flat ride without even a stop sign all the way to the village of Chelsea. At mile 1.5 note Parker Road on your left.

- **OPTIONAL PARKER ROAD ROUTE,** 7 miles one way, links to Manchester or into Ann Arbor. Shortly after exiting the village you will come to Parker Road, which only heads south. This lovely road will take you past Dexter

Highlights on your way into Chelsea include the home of Jiffy Mix as well as the clock tower, once the tallest building in the county.

High School and after 7 miles to a four-way stop on Scio Church Road. From there you can go straight and head farther south on Parker, turn left (east) and head into Ann Arbor, or turn right (west) and head toward M-52. These choices are described as part of the Manchester Ride (p. 61). ❖

The speed limit increases on this portion of Dexter-Chelsea Road, but there is usually little traffic to interfere with a lovely ride. Enjoy the occasional wildflowers as the road bends gently uphill left and then right at mile 2.4. At mile 5.3 you pass a mill and again pass over the railroad tracks; note that there are several sets of tracks. The scenery opens up as you closely track the railroad tracks and can enjoy the fields on either side. You may occasionally see sandhill cranes feeding in the fields along this road—the cranes are striking birds that stand up to five feet tall with long, thin legs.

You are now nearing Chelsea (see map, p. 26), a small town originally settled in the 1830s. As you enter the town there is new housing and then a cemetery on your left. Soon coming into view will be the Jiffy Mix structure, part of the family-owned Chelsea Milling

Company, which has been in business for over one hundred years. You can also see the European-style, seven-story clock tower, built in 1907 as the home of the Glazier Stove Works. Standing 135 feet tall, it was once the tallest building in Washtenaw County. The building is now undergoing renovation and restoration intended to restore it to its original appearance of a century ago.

At mile 7.9 turn left (south) on McKinley Road, noting that while you have a stop sign the cross traffic does not. On your right you will see the Chelsea Depot, a train station originally built only for freight, which carried wool, grain, apples, and meat from nearby farms. The station's appearance was upgraded in 1880 to give it a somewhat Victorian flavor. Regular train service was discontinued in 1981.

Cross the railroad tracks, then turn quickly right (west) onto Middle Street at mile 8.0. At mile 8.2 you come to Main Street and a selection of coffee shops. Water and toilets are available at the police station on Middle Street. Bicycles are a common sight here, and the

RIDING WITH EQUIPMENT

There is certainly no shortage of equipment with which one can ride. At a bare minimum, you should be prepared to change a flat tire—as you are eventually going to have one. You will need a replacement tube (and perhaps a patch kit), tire irons (if you don't need them, you don't need to read this section), and a means of inflating the tire, with either a pump or a CO_2 cartridge. The CO_2 cartridge will work rapidly and easily, but when it's done it's done. A pump is a little more difficult to carry and won't get the tire as fully inflated, but it will work over and over again (or until you get tired). Before putting on the new tube, be sure to check inside the tire for the cause of the flat or else your next tube may immediately go flat. Obviously, you will need to know how to change the tire, an art best practiced at home.

While they are not exactly "equipment," you should always ride with at least a couple of other things. One is some cash. You may need it to get a bite to eat or to make a phone call if you need a ride. Better still is a cell phone, although it may not work in some areas. The other is some form of identification. One can hope you will never need it, but you ought to have something on you or your bike that says who you are in the event that you can't.

AABTS has placed bike racks for the many people who come to ride. This is the end of the Dexter-Chelsea route, but it is one end of the Waterloo Loop as well as one end of the Ride to Hell.

ROUTE CUES:

0.0   Start at the corner of Mast Road and Huron River Drive, Dexter. Go south on Mast Road into Dexter.
0.2   Turn right (west) on Huron.
0.3   Turn left (south) on Broad Street.
0.6   Turn right (northwest) on 5th Street. The road turns left (south) and becomes Alpine Road.
0.8   Turn right (northwest) on Main Street.
0.9   Turn left (southwest) on Dexter-Chelsea Road.
1.5   Note Parker Road on the left.
5.3   Cross railroad tracks.
7.9   Turn left (south) on McKinley Road. Cross railroad tracks again.
8.0   Turn right (west) on Middle Street.
8.2   Corner of Main Street and Middle Street, Chelsea.

"So ardent a cyclist must be full of energy."
Arthur Conan Doyle,
"The Adventure of the Solitary Cyclist"

*W*aterloo Loop

ROUTE: Loop from downtown Chelsea, 18 miles

LINKS WITH: Dexter-Chelsea Road
Ride to Hell

OPTIONS: Ridge Road Loop

PARKING: Street parking and free parking lots are available
in Chelsea.

*This ride takes you through parts of the Waterloo Recreation Area
and can feature wildlife as well as some hills.*

Start at the corner of Middle Street and Main Street in Chelsea, where
a map on the south side of Zou Zou's coffee shop gives a sketch of
roads in the Waterloo area. Feel free to follow this route on that map
or make your own route!

From the corner of Middle Street and Main Street go west on
Middle Street. At mile 0.7 the road turns right (briefly becoming
Cleveland Street) and then left over the railroad tracks at the site of
the Chelsea United Methodist Retirement Communities, founded
in 1906 and still quite active today. Head west on Cavanaugh Lake
Road, with the train tracks on your left, past tall grasses and wetlands
where you can occasionally see some interesting wildfowl. You will
pass Cavanaugh Lake on your right, along with a group of lakefront
cottages and a small park. Immediately thereafter, at mile 4.5, you will
pass Ridge Road.

- **OPTIONAL RIDGE ROAD LOOP,** 11.0 miles from the center of Chelsea and
  back. If you want to cut the length of the Waterloo Loop roughly in half,

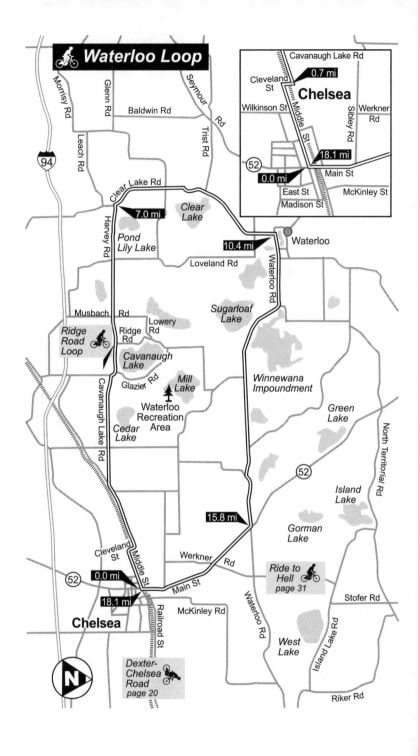

turn right (north) on Ridge Road, which runs along the western shore of Cavanaugh Lake. Turn right (east) on Glazier Road and come back round the lake to Cavanaugh Lake Road; a left turn (east) will take you back into Chelsea. ❖

At mile 6.1 you will enter Jackson County, named after former president Andrew Jackson. The road becomes Harvey Road, and at mile 7.0 you will come to a T intersection with Clear Lake Road.

Turn right (north) onto Clear Lake Road and enjoy a ride through the Waterloo Recreation Area, the largest park in Michigan's Lower Peninsula. Shaped by glaciers long ago, the park offers a wide range of recreational activities, including camping, trails for hikers and horses, and cross-country skiing in the winter.

At mile 8.9 you will come upon Trist Road on the left, which can lead to some pleasant riding not covered in this book. Sandhill cranes nest in the area. They stand about five feet tall, with long thin legs. Sandhill cranes nest in the brush but are often seen feeding in open fields. In 2007 a rare whooping crane made an appearance in the usual group of sandhill cranes.

RIDING IN COLD WEATHER

Michigan can get cold. If you plan to ride year-round, it will help to keep a log of winds and temperatures to see what clothing combination works best for you. If you are feeling quite warm and comfortable after one mile, you are very likely to be taking off layers soon thereafter, so you will need to plan for what you are going to do with the layers you take off. Your feet and face are likely to be the most difficult parts of your body to keep warm. If there is ice on the road, remember that whether you can control your bike is only one part of the safety equation. Another is the question of whether the drivers passing you can control their cars! Especially beware of ice on railroad tracks, which can make your bike impossible to control.

But don't give up on riding between November and April. There are winter days in Michigan when the temperature becomes quite pleasant, especially when combined with the body heat generated by a bike ride. The scenery is also quite different from that in the summer when the lush greenery can obscure views of nearby rivers or faraway vistas.

You sweat even in cold weather. Keep drinking.

A deer crossing Huron River Drive on a January day

At mile 10.4 you will come to a T intersection with Waterloo Road. There is a small restaurant on your left if you are feeling hungry.

Turn right (east) and enjoy another stretch through the recreation area; the undulating hills make the ride interesting and might make you sweat. A little less than two miles after the turn you will see Mill Lake Bread on your right, an excellent place to stop for a snack. At mile 14.4 you will pass the Cassidy Lake Special Incarceration Facility, and at mile 15.8 you will reach highway M-52. Turn right (south). The road is busy, but there is a wide shoulder to ride on and it's mostly downhill. After about a mile note the sharply angled Werkner Road on the left, which links with the Ride to Hell. At mile 18.1 you are back where you started.

ROUTE CUES:

0.0   Start at the corner of Middle Street and Main Street, Chelsea.
      Go west.

0.7	Turn right (north) over railroad tracks on Cleveland Street and then immediately left (west) on Cavanaugh Lake Road.
4.5	Ridge Road, on the right (north), is the start of the optional Ridge Road Loop.
6.1	Cavanaugh Road becomes Harvey Road.
7.0	Turn right (north) on Clear Lake Road.
10.4	Turn right (east) on Waterloo Road.
15.8	Turn right (south) on M-52.
18.1	Arrive back at the start in Chelsea.

RIDING IN WET WEATHER

Michigan can get wet. Riding in wet weather poses challenges in terms of both dress and safe riding. Obviously, appropriate rain gear is essential. Roads are particularly slick immediately after the rain begins, as oil and dust float to the surface of the water. Beware painted lines and steel surfaces, as they can be significantly slicker in the rain than the rest of the road. Avoid puddles, as you don't know how deep a hole underneath might be. Slightly decreasing your tire pressure may help you gain a little more traction on wet surfaces. Grip your brakes slowly, as this may brush water away from the tire and help the brake grip better. But be cognizant that stopping distances will be longer no matter what you do. You are also more likely to have a flat tire, as glass and other items tend to stick to the tire. After you get home, stuffing newspaper in your shoes can hasten the drying process.

"*I was not yet sixteen when I understood a great deal, from having ridden bicycles for so long, about style, speed, grace, purpose, value, form, integrity, health, humor, music, breathing, and finally and perhaps the best of all the relationship between the beginning and the end.*"

William Saroyan, *The Bicycle Rider in Beverly Hills*

$\mathscr{R}$IDE TO HELL

ROUTE: Chelsea to Hell to Hudson Mills Metropark,
        22.1 miles

LINKS WITH: Huron River Drive, North Territorial Extension
            Dexter-Chelsea Road
            Waterloo Loop
            East Lansing

PARKING: Street parking and free parking lots are available
          in downtown Chelsea and the Hudson Mills
          Metropark.

Hell, Michigan, can be approached from a number of directions. For a bike rider that number is two. The road to Hell does not appear to be paved with good intentions; it is paved with asphalt, just like all the other roads in the area. Feel free to insert any other of many bad jokes that have been made about this town . . .

This route takes you from the lovely village of Chelsea to Hell, Michigan. Head north out of town on M-52/Main Street, a busy road but one that has nice, wide shoulders on which to ride. After only 1.3 miles you turn right (northeast) onto Werkner Road and immediately enter an area of gently rolling hills and houses. This is part of the annual ride sponsored by the Ann Arbor Bicycle Touring Society, "One Helluva Ride," and if you look closely you can usually see sketches of pitchforks on the road marking the route. At mile 3.6

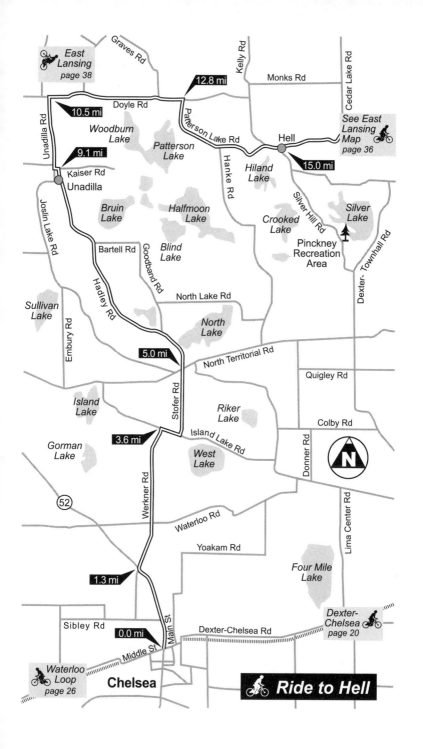

Hell, Michigan, can be a very friendly place to visit.

make a bending right-hand turn (east) onto Island Lake Road, followed at 4.0 by a left (north) onto Stofer Road. (You are basically just following the paved road around.)

At 5.0 cross North Territorial Road (with care as cars can be moving fast), and Stofer Road becomes Hadley Road. Ride past lakes and up and down some rolling hills through the Pinckney State Recreation Area, home to the excellent mountain-biking Potawatomi Trail, as well as some nice hiking trails. You pass a Boy Scout Camp at mile 7.9. At mile 9.0 you come to the Unadilla Cemetery and cross into Livingston County, named for President Andrew Jackson's secretary of state, Edward Livingston. You soon come to the small and pleasantly named community of Unadilla. Wind through the town, passing the Unadilla Grocery Store, making a left for a very short stretch on Kaiser Road, and then turning right and continuing north on Unadilla Road. At mile 10.5 turn right (east) onto Doyle Road, also called Michigan road D-32. The road is densely wooded for a while but then opens up into an area with more houses. At mile 12.3 the University of Michigan Edwin S. George Reserve is on the left, the site of many long- and short-term biological studies. At mile 12.8 the paved road becomes Patterson Lake Road. There are some nice hills there, but be careful of potholes.

At mile 15.0 ride over Hell Creek and you have arrived in Hell. Stand in front of the sign and take a picture or have your picture taken. Ponder where it is, indeed, hotter than Hell. Contemplate whether it is a cold day in Hell and what that implies for your life's choices. Visit one of the three businesses, buy a souvenir, have a snack or a meal at the Dam Site Inn, or just have one Hell of a time.

When you have had your fill of Hell, continue down the road. After a short stretch, in which the road going straight ahead changes to Darwin Road, at mile 17.6 turn right (south) onto Dexter-Pinckney Road. Follow the road south as at mile 19.6 it winds its way between two lakes that are a popular place for water sports in the summer. At mile 21.8 you will come to North Territorial Road.

Turn left (east), taking care on this busy road. You will cross over the Huron River and arrive at Hudson Mills Metropark on your right. Alternatively, you can continue on a few hundred yards and turn right (south) onto Huron River Drive, which can link to rides to Ann Arbor, Dexter, or back to Chelsea.

RIDING IN HOT WEATHER

Michigan can get hot. When it does, it's essential to replenish the fluid you sweat away. Drink regularly. Think about taking a drink every ten to fifteen minutes whether you feel particularly thirsty or not. On a hot day you can be losing a significant amount of fluid without being aware of it. Biking clothes don't absorb the sweat, and it quickly evaporates in the breeze created by riding. By the time you feel appreciably thirsty you may be quite significantly in need of fluid. It is best not to get to that point.

Freezing a water bottle (or two) can help provide you with cool water, at least until it heats up! When putting the bottle in your freezer, remember that the water will expand as it freezes, so leave some air space at the top of the bottle. Some people find that carrying water on their backs and drinking through a tube helps to keep up the fluids. Some riders find a sports drink such as Gatorade a good option in addition to or instead of drinking water. If you can, learn to drink while riding, but be sure to maintain control of the bike.

ROUTE CUES:

0.0   Start at the corner of Middle Street and Main Street, Chelsea. Head north on Main Street/M-52.

1.3   Turn right (northeast) on Werkner Road.

3.6   Turn right (east) on Island Lake Road.

4.0   Turn left (north) on Stofer Road.

5.0   Cross North Territorial Road. Stofer Road becomes Hadley Road.

9.1   Turn left on Kaiser Road, then immediately right on Unadilla Road.

10.5   Turn right (east) on Doyle Road.

12.8   Doyle Road becomes Patterson Lake Road.

15.0   Arrive in Hell.

17.0   Go straight as the road becomes Darwin Road.

17.6   Turn right (south) on Dexter-Pinckney Road.

21.8   Turn left (east) on North Territorial Road.

22.1   Turn right (south) into Hudson Mills Metropark.

"Bicycling . . . is the nearest approximation I know to the flight of birds."
Louis J. Halle Jr., *Spring in Washington*

$\mathcal{E}$AST LANSING

ROUTE: Ann Arbor (Wheeler Park) to East Lansing
(Livestock Pavilion), 61.7 miles

LINKS WITH: Huron River Drive, North Territorial Extension
Ride to Hell

PARKING: Street parking is available near Wheeler Park, Ann
Arbor. Note that there is sometimes a time limit on
street parking. Parking is available at the Livestock
Pavilion, East Lansing.

*This pleasant ride can take the rider from Ann Arbor to East
Lansing, the towns that are home to the two largest universities in
the state. Starting in Ann Arbor, the ride is almost sixty-two miles
long, so most people will not want to ride both ways in a single day.
The ride goes through a diverse range of sceneries and can provide
a real feeling of accomplishment at the end.*

For the first part of the ride, take Huron River Drive and the optional
extension to North Territorial Road. See pages 9–18 for a description.
You will pass Hudson Mills Metropark, but if you are going all the
way to East Lansing you probably won't be stopping for long. (As an
alternative, you can drive to Hudson Mills Metropark and ride from
there.) This ride description starts at the end of the North Territorial
Road Extension to Huron River Drive, mile 13.6, at the corner of
Huron River Drive and North Territorial Road.

At North Territorial Road—a busy road, take care!—turn left
(west) and then right (north) onto Dexter-Pinckney Road at mile 14.3.
At mile 16.0 you will see McGregor Road on your right and will start
to pass between two lakes. At certain times of the year this will be a

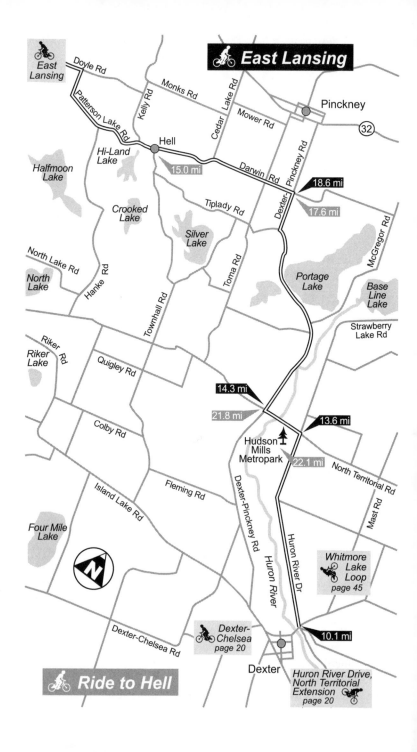

East Lansing

Doyle Rd

Monks Rd

Cedar Lake Rd

Mower Rd

Pinckney

(32)

Patterson Lake Rd

Kelly Rd

Hell

Hi-Land Lake

Darwin Rd

Pinckney Rd

18.6 mi

Halfmoon Lake

Crooked Lake

Tiplady Rd

17.6 mi

15.0 mi

Silver Lake

McGregor Rd

North Lake Rd

Hanke Rd

Toma Rd

Portage Lake

Base Line Lake

North Lake

Townhall Rd

Strawberry Lake Rd

Riker Rd

Riker Lake

Quigley Rd

14.3 mi

21.8 mi

13.6 mi

Colby Rd

Hudson Mills Metropark

22.1 mi

North Territorial Rd

Island Lake Rd

Fleming Rd

Dexter-Pinckney Rd

Mast Rd

Four Mile Lake

Huron River Dr

Whitmore Lake Loop page 45

Huron River

10.1 mi

Dexter-Chelsea Rd

Dexter-Chelsea page 20

Dexter

N

Ride to Hell

Huron River Drive, North Territorial Extension page 20

RIDING WITH CARS: CLOTHING AND BEING SEEN

There are two primary considerations in choosing clothes for biking: comfort and safety. The most important safety item for riding with cars is to be seen, to be visible. Road-riding jerseys accomplish that task in many ways. Bright colors are one. Reflective fabric is another; it really works, and if you are ever caught riding as the light drops you will be very happy to become a brightly illuminated object in the eyes of drivers! Riding at night requires lights, both front and rear. Remember that you want drivers to see you, and you must do whatever is necessary to accomplish that goal.

RIDING WITH CARS: WHERE AND HOW

Another aspect of coexisting with cars that can make the experience more pleasant for all is the choice of where to ride. You shouldn't and needn't ride too close to the curb—the pavement is often broken there, and you give yourself less margin for error. Michigan law says, in fact, that bicyclists are to "ride as near to the right side of the roadway as practicable," and one might logically surmise that this means you need not ride so close to the edge as to put your safety at risk. Michigan law also says that you can ride two abreast, but it's best to use some common sense and move over when there are cars approaching from the rear. The same goes for large groups of bicyclists on the road. Drivers who get irritated at bicyclists when a group won't move over will probably be irritated the next time they come across a bicyclist on a county ride. It's better to just be polite.

Finally, wearing earphones is always a bad idea. Much of the information you need when riding comes from sound, and anything that inhibits your ability to get that information is going to make your ride less safe.

road busy with vacationers headed to and from their summer homes on these lakes. At mile 17.4 you enter Livingston County.

At mile 18.6 you turn left (west) onto Darwin Road, which is marked by a white fence on the north side of the road and a sign pointing to the town of Hell. Head toward Hell. The road quickly

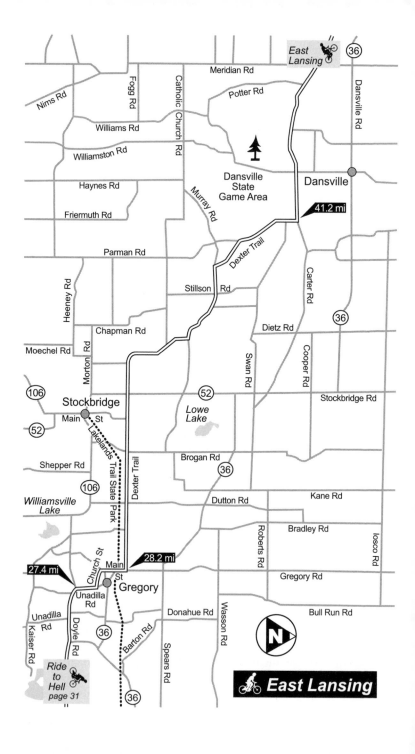

Horses enjoying the afternoon along the road to East Lansing

becomes Patterson Lake Road/D-32 at mile 19.1, and shortly after entering the Pinckney Recreation Area, at mile 21.1, you will find that you truly are in Hell.

You may not wish to tarry in Hell at this time, as you still have a long way to go. Continue through town on the paved road, which after a time will become Doyle Road. (Please reference map on page 38 now.) At mile 25.7 you will see Unadilla Road on your left, followed soon after by a grass landing strip that is often used for glider flights. Follow the paved road north as it becomes Unadilla Road, Church Street, and then Main Street as you approach the town of Gregory at mile 27.4.

Lakelands Trail State Park crosses the road at this point. The park is a linear rails-to-trails park that runs from Stockbridge to Pinckney. It has the advantage of no cars and level terrain, but the surface is broken up (at least at the time of this writing) to the extent that it is best ridden on a mountain bike. A convenience store on your right and some nice shaded benches on the left make this a pleasant place to stop. Via this route you are about to start a stretch of over twenty

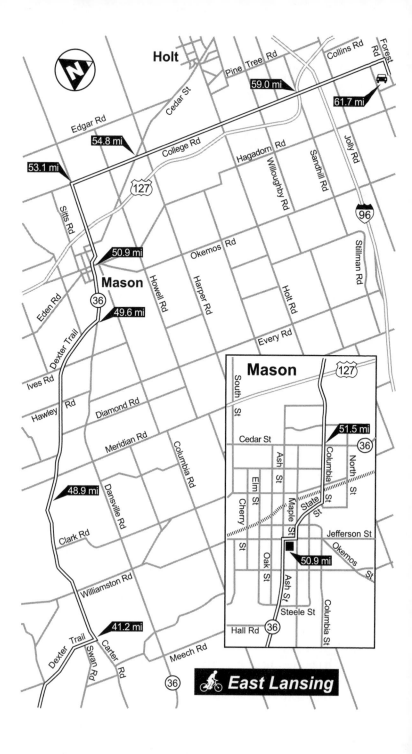

Holt

N

59.0 mi
61.7 mi

Pine Tree Rd
Collins Rd
Forest Rd

Cedar St
Edgar Rd
College Rd
Hagadorn Rd
Willoughby Rd
Sandhill Rd
Jolly Rd

54.8 mi
53.1 mi

127
Sitts Rd

96

50.9 mi

Mason
36

49.6 mi

Eden Rd
Dexter Trail
Howell Rd
Harper Rd
Okemos Rd
Holt Rd
Stillman Rd

Every Rd

Ives Rd
Hawley Rd
Diamond Rd
Meridian Rd
Columbia Rd
Dansville Rd

48.9 mi

Clark Rd

Williamston Rd

41.2 mi

Dexter Trail
Swan Rd
Carter Rd
Meech Rd

36

Mason   127

South St
Cedar St
Ash St
Elm St
Cherry St
Oak St
Ash St
Maple St
State St
Columbia St
North St
51.5 mi
36
Jefferson St
Okemos St
50.9 mi
Steele St
Hall Rd
Columbia St
36

🚴 *East Lansing*

The town square around Mason's courthouse is a nice place for a brief rest.

miles during which you won't have another opportunity to get food and water, so now would be a good time to assess your supplies and stock up if you need to.

Continue north out of Gregory on Main Street. At mile 28.2 turn left (west) onto Dexter Trail and settle in for some lovely rolling hills. Here and elsewhere you will find evidence that you are sharing the road with horses and other farm animals. At mile 31.1 you enter Ingham County, and at mile 32.9 you will see Main Street on your left, which leads to the village of Stockbridge. Our route bypasses Stockbridge and remains on Dexter Trail. (If you need to visit this small town, which has plenty of shops, it is only about a mile down the road.)

Continue along Dexter Trail as it crosses highway M-52 at mile 33.6 and then winds its way in a generally northwesterly direction. The road will twist and turn, but stay on Dexter Trail, which is the most obvious paved route. At mile 41.2 you will come to a T intersection with Carter Road; turn left (west), which will keep you on Dexter

Trail. (Please reference map on page 40 now.) At mile 48.9 you will see an airport on the left, and at mile 49.6 you will come to a T intersection with M-36. Turn left (west) and enter the village of Mason as M-36 becomes Ash Street.

At mile 50.9 you come to the town square and the Mason City Courthouse, a rather stately Romanesque building with lovely trees, which is on the National Register of Historic Places. The square is a nice place to relax. When you are ready to leave, continue past the town square and turn right (north) on Jefferson Street and then left (west) on Maple. In the next block Maple angles right (northwest) to become State Street. It then veers left (west) to become Columbia Street. Continue west on Columbia as you cross Cedar Street at mile 51.5 and then pass over the expressway (M-127).

At mile 53.1 turn right on College Road, which provides you with a straight shot up to East Lansing. There is occasionally some quite generous shoulder, and the road is frequently traveled by bicyclists, often coming from East Lansing. You will cross Cedar Street (again) at mile 54.8, and at mile 59.0 you will pass under M-127 (again) and then over I-96. At mile 60.1 you will reach Jolly Road and begin to see smokestacks on the Michigan State University campus, originally Michigan Agricultural College. Enjoy riding amid the farms that are part of the first institution of higher learning in United States to teach scientific agriculture. The dairy cattle teaching and research buildings are on your left. At mile 61.7 you reach Forest Road at the southern border of the campus. Turn right (east) and then left (north) into the parking lot at the Pavilion for Agriculture and Livestock Education, which is located at the northeast corner of College Road and Forest Road.

ROUTE CUES:

0.0   Start at Wheeler Park, Ann Arbor. Follow the routes for Huron River Drive and the North Territorial Extension to mile 13.6 (see pages 9–18).

13.6   Turn left (west) on North Territorial Road.

14.3   Turn right (north) on Dexter-Pinckney Road.

18.6   Turn left (west) on Darwin Road, which becomes first Patterson Lake Road and then Doyle Road.

27.4   The road turns right (north) and becomes Unadilla Road, Church Street, and Main Street.

28.2   Turn left (west) on Dexter Trail.

41.2   Turn left (Dexter Trail continues).

49.6   Turn left (northwest) on M-36, which becomes Ash Street. Enter Mason.

50.9   Turn right (north) on Jefferson Street.

51.0   Turn left (west) on Maple Street, which becomes State Street and Columbia Street.

53.1   Turn right (north) on College Road.

61.7   Turn right (east) on Forest Road and then left (north) into the pavilion parking lot in East Lansing.

BIKE RIDES WHEN THE BIKE DOESN'T

Some of these rides take you into fairly rural territory. Sooner or later you are going to wind up in a situation in which your bike suffers an irreparable breakdown, at least one you can't fix on the road, and you will be standing by the side of the road with a bike that will not ride. It's always a good idea to carry a (charged) cell phone and some change for a phone call in case you get stuck away from cell phone reception, as well as phone numbers that could help you get home. Don't hesitate to ask for help, especially from other bicyclists. There's a fairly strong implicit code of conduct such that most bicyclists will gladly stop to help. They might well have what you need to get you rolling again.

> *"Bikes talk to each other like dogs, they wag their wheels and tinkle their bells, the riders let their mounts mingle."*
>
> Daniel Behrman, *The Man Who Loved Bicycles*

*W*HITMORE LAKE LOOP

ROUTE: Dexter, the corner of Huron River Drive and Mast Road, to Ann Arbor, Wheeler Park, 24.3 miles

LINKS WITH: Huron River Drive
Dexter-Chelsea Road

OPTIONS: 7 Mile Road to Pontiac Trail
Warren Road to Pontiac Trail
Alternate route back through Bandemer Park

PARKING: Street parking is available in downtown Dexter and around Wheeler Park in Ann Arbor.

This loop provides an alternate route from Dexter back into Ann Arbor with a few hills, a lake, and a nice, long downhill to finish it off. If you do the route in reverse it also makes a nice ride out of Ann Arbor north to Whitmore Lake.

From the intersection of Huron River Drive and Mast Road near Dexter, head north on Mast Road. The terrain has a few stair-stepping hills but nothing too onerous as you ride a somewhat curving road past fields and houses and some very nice scenic views. The traffic can be busy and cars a bit fast at times. Around mile 2.0, just beyond Gregory Road, look for a charming farmhouse on the left, at 6015 Mast Road, built around 1860 in the Greek revival style.

After crossing North Territorial Road at mile 3.0 you start to see more fields and fewer houses and even a few horses. At mile 5.8 there is a T intersection at Strawberry Lake Road. Although you can't see them just yet, you are now and will remain in the vicinity of many small lakes for some time. Turn right (east) and soon enter Livingston

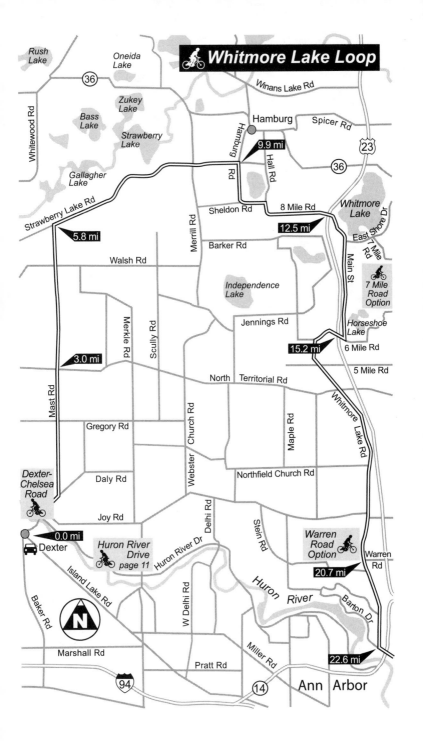

Boats await a pleasant day on Whitmore Lake

County at mile 6.1. The environment comes to include more houses and fewer farms. At the first stop sign since you turned onto Strawberry Lake Road, turn right on Hamburg Road at mile 9.9; there will be a cemetery ahead and on the left as you make the turn. For the next few miles follow the main paved road as it turns left and then right. As you head in a southeasterly direction, the name of the road changes (although it is not always well marked). From Hamburg Road bear left onto Sheldon Road, then Hall Road, and finally 8 Mile Road.

Numbered mile roads such as 8 Mile Road are a reminder of the early days of the republic. Named long before Michigan became a state, these roads are derived from surveys conducted to organize what was then the Northwest Territory. The baseline for the survey was 8 Mile Road. The road lies about eight miles north of downtown Detroit and serves as the dividing line between Detroit and its northern suburbs, as well as the title of a famous movie starring the rapper Eminem. But none of that is obvious here at the far western end of 8 Mile Road. Interrupted by Whitmore Lake on its way east, 8 Mile Road goes almost all the way to Lake St. Clair.

As you work your way around the lakes in the area, stay on the main, paved road. At mile 12.0 you reenter Washtenaw County and cross some railroad tracks.

At mile 12.5 as you pass over the expressway (US-23) Whitmore Lake comes into view. Called the "most beautiful lake in Michigan" by admirers in 1841, it was formed by retreating glaciers some twelve thousand years ago. For many years it was a major vacation spot for Ann Arbor residents. A toll road once ran between Ann Arbor and Whitmore Lake, and the first bicycle path in Washtenaw County was opened between the two towns in 1897. Today the toll road is gone and one has a choice between the expressway and Whitmore Lake Road, at which you will shortly arrive.

As you pass the lake on your left, 8 Mile Road turns south and becomes Main Street, where one can stop at any of a wide range of shops that cater to the many people who enjoy lakefront homes. There is a convenient, pleasant, and well-stocked gas station at the stoplight at East Shore Drive if all you want is a snack.

- **OPTIONAL 7 MILE ROAD TO PONTIAC TRAIL route,** 7 miles. If you want to ride farther east you can continue around the southern edge of the lake and up the eastern side to get to 7 Mile Road. Turn left at the stoplight onto East Shore Drive and then right onto 7 Mile Road. Take 7 Mile Road 5.6 miles east to link with the Pontiac Trail route. ❖

Follow Main Street south. After crossing the railroad tracks, at a sign that reads "Athletic Field," Gloria's Fine Home Cooking restaurant is just west of Main Street. You get a few glimpses of Horseshoe Lake on your left (which on a map does look like a horseshoe with some use of the imagination). Traffic can be a bit busy here. At 6 Mile Road, mile 15.2, turn right (west) and go back over the expressway (US-23). Soon you will come to Whitmore Lake Road, at which point the environment becomes a good deal less commercial and the road relatively lightly traveled. Turn left (south) onto Whitmore Lake Road at mile 15.6. At mile 17.1 you cross North Territorial Road and acquire a reasonable shoulder. The ride into Ann Arbor is mostly downhill from there. You can see US-23 on your left; during rush hour have a look at the slow-moving cars and be glad you're enjoying a bicycle ride! At mile 18.8 you pass Saint Patrick's Church on your right, the oldest English-speaking Catholic parish in the state.

- **OPTIONAL WARREN ROAD TO PONTIAC TRAIL route,** 1 mile. At mile 20.7 you can take Warren Road east to link with the Pontiac Trail route. ❖

At mile 22.6 you come to the end of Whitmore Lake Road at its intersection with Barton Drive.

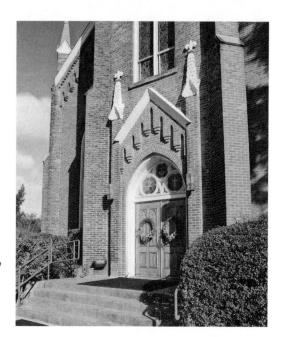

Saint Patrick's Church on Whitmore Lake Road, the oldest English-speaking parish in the state

- **OPTIONAL ALTERNATE ROUTE BACK THROUGH BANDEMER PARK.** A slower but more scenic way to come into Ann Arbor from the end of Whitmore Lake Road (mile 22.6) is to go straight over the Huron River into Bandemer Park. A bike path (also used by pedestrians, Rollerbladers, and others—take care!) goes south with the river on your left. This is a stretch of riding that leaves you amazed that you can be so close to the center of town and yet seem so far out in the country! After a mile the path will turn left (east) and cross the Huron River atop the Argo Dam; walk your bike over this narrow path. You then enter a dirt parking lot and make a quick right turn onto the first paved road, Long Shore Drive, which will bring you to the foot of Pontiac Trail. Turn right onto Pontiac Trail and rejoin the main route immediately before the bridge over the Huron River. Total mileage is about the same for both routes. ❖

Turn left (east) on Barton Drive. At mile 23.2 turn right (south) on Pontiac Trail. After less than a mile you will make a sharp, very short left turn on Swift Street and come to Broadway Street at mile 24.0, on which you can turn right (south) to go over the bridge and back into the center of Ann Arbor. Immediately upon exiting the bridge turn right on Summit Street at mile 24.2 to bring you to Wheeler Park in only one more block.

0.0   Start at the corner of Mast Road and Huron River Drive, Dexter. Go north on Mast Road.

3.0   Cross North Territorial Road.

5.8   Turn right (east) on Strawberry Lake Road.

6.1   Enter Livingston County.

9.9   Turn right (south) on Hamburg Road. Follow the paved road as it becomes Sheldon Road, Hall Road, and then 8 Mile Road.

12.0   Enter Washtenaw County.

12.5   Pass over an expressway (US-23).

13.0   8 Mile Road becomes Main Street.

15.2   Turn right (east) on 6 Mile Road.

15.6   Turn left (south) on Whitmore Lake Road.

17.1   Cross North Territorial Road.

20.7   Continue on Whitmore Lake Road. Note Warren Road on your left.

22.6   Turn left (east) on Barton Drive.

23.2   Turn right (south) on Pontiac Trail.

23.9   Turn left (west) on Swift Street.

24.0   Turn right (south) on Broadway Street.

24.2   Turn right (west) on Summit Street.

24.3   Arrive at Wheeler Park.

> *"He knew the road by heart . . . he knew that road by feel and by sight, as one knows a living body, and he rode expertly along it, pressing resilient pedals into a rustling void."*
>
> Vladimir Nabokov, *Mary*

$\mathscr{D}$ixboro Road

ROUTE: Loop beginning at the eastern end of Gallup Park, Ann Arbor, 23.8 miles

LINKS WITH: Pontiac Trail (optional return)
               Whitmore Lake Loop (via the 7 Mile Road Option)

PARKING: Parking is available at the eastern end of Gallup Park.

This loop goes generally uphill for several miles, after which you have the option of coming back into Ann Arbor or continuing through fields and horse farms.

The route starts at the eastern end of Gallup Park, near the Geddes Dam on the Huron River, where the river's energy was once used to generate hydroelectric power. Immediately to the east is Parker Mill Park, which still houses a functioning gristmill and a cider mill dating from the late 1800s, as well as some nature trails. The park could be a relaxing stop before or after your ride. This was once the hamlet of Geddesburg and in 1824 the site of the first sawmill in Washtenaw County, which benefited in 1839 from the arrival of the Michigan Central Railroad.

On leaving the park turn left (north) on an unmarked road to pass over the river. You are paralleling and below Dixboro Road, which is the larger bridge immediately to your right. Go up the hill and after about 100 yards take a brief jog to the right and then the left to join Dixboro Road, taking care as there can be traffic. Ride up Dixboro Road, heading north away from the river and generally uphill. You will immediately cross Geddes Road and at mile 1.0 you will pass the NSF on the left. Although the National Science Foundation is a prominent

Heading north on Dixboro Road

funder of much research at the University of Michigan, this is another NSF, founded in 1944 as the National Standards Foundation and known for developing standards for public health, safety, and environmental protection. At mile 2.4 you will pass the University of Michigan's Matthaei Botanical Gardens. The gardens offer several outdoor trails (for walking only) through terrain that evokes the natural prairies. There is also a pleasant indoor setting. At mile 3.0 you cross Plymouth Road, acquiring a nice shoulder, and at mile 3.9 you pass over an expressway (M-14). Enjoy the brief downhill ride, as it's followed by a series of stair-stepping hills past fields and a few houses up to the intersection with Pontiac Trail at mile 6.5.

- **OPTION:** Turn left and head south down the Pontiac Trail route back to Ann Arbor. If you do this on a late fall afternoon, take care, as the sun may be directly ahead of you and the glare not only makes it difficult to see the road but also difficult for drivers to see you. If you wish to return to your starting point at Gallup Park, follow the Pontiac Trail route (in reverse) but go past Fuller Park and its swimming pool on your left and Mitchell Park on your right. Immediately after passing Mitchell Field turn right onto the sidewalk and follow it across the river to the western end of Gallup Park. From this point follow the Gallup Park bike path the 3 miles back to your starting point at the eastern end of the park. ❖

The main route goes north into a region of fields and horse farms. Turn right (north) onto Pontiac Trail. After crossing North Territorial Road at mile 6.8, the next few miles take you past a combination of fields and farms, some with beautiful vistas, some with horses, and many with both. There can be quite a few cars on this road during rush hour.

At mile 10.4 turn right (east) onto 7 Mile Road; there is a convenience store here if you want to grab a snack. If you prefer, continue up the road to the outskirts of the town of South Lyon. At this point there is a wider selection of shops, but the traffic becomes progressively more severe as you head into town.

- **OPTION:** Turn left on 7 Mile Road and follow it for 5.6 miles to link to the Whitmore Lake Loop. ❖

Ride past a mix of houses and farms and continue on Angle Road at mile 11.5. Despite the name, Angle Road goes straight while 7 Mile Road turns to the left! At mile 12.5 turn left (east) on Six Mile Road and quickly turn right (south) on Curtis Road. When you reach North Territorial Road at mile 15.2 note the Jarvis Stone School House on your right. Built in 1857 of local stones and boulders, this one-room schoolhouse was in continuous use until 1967. It has been restored and is now used by the Salem Area Historical Society.

At mile 17.2 pass over the expressway (M-14) and at mile 17.5 reach Plymouth Road, a busier road than you have encountered to this point, which offers an adequate if not inspiring surface for a ride back into Ann Arbor. Turn right (west) and be glad for the generous shoulder.

This section of road does offer some interesting historical sites, which are well documented in one of the driving tours published by the Washtenaw County Historic Preservation Project. Shortly after making the turn look on your right for the Geer-Staebler Farm at 7734 Plymouth Road. Once a nineteenth-century subsistence farm, it, like many in the area, later became a commercial dairy farm.

You soon enter Frain's Lake, founded in 1835. At 7500 Plymouth Road note the attractive Italianate school with a cute steeple on the left, constructed in 1872. At mile 18.7 cross highway M-153 where, alas, the shoulder disappears. At 6595 Plymouth Road note a house, built between 1856 and 1864, that is said to be one of the most elegant Greek revival houses in the area, although at present it looks a bit in need of repair. At mile 20.0 you pass Ford Road and soon thereafter enter Dixboro, founded in 1824 by Captain John Dix. An interesting historical sketch on the Web site of the Dixboro General Store

Grazing horses reflected in a pond on Pontiac Trail

(founded in 1840) describes how this small community was at one point poised to outstrip Ann Arbor for pride of place in Washtenaw County. However, the railroad line was sited some miles to the south, the founder decamped for Texas in 1833, and Dixboro has remained a small community. The Dixboro United Methodist Church on your right, another Greek revival structure, was built in 1858 and is listed on the National Register of Historic Places. At mile 20.8 you return to the corner of Dixboro Road, mile 3.0 at the start of this ride, from which point you can turn left (south) and return to Gallup Park.

ROUTE CUES:

- 0.0   Start at the eastern end of Gallup Park, Ann Arbor.
- 3.0   Cross Plymouth Road.
- 3.9   Pass over an expressway (M-14).
- 6.5   Turn right (north) on Pontiac Trail.
- 8.8   Cross North Territorial Road.
- 10.4   Turn right (east) on 7 Mile Road.
- 11.5   The road becomes Angle Road (go straight).
- 12.5   Turn left (east) on 6 Mile Road.

12.6	Turn right (south) on Curtis Road.
15.2	Cross North Territorial Road.
17.2	Pass over the expressway (M-14).
17.5	Turn right (west) on Plymouth Road.
20.8	Turn left (south) on Dixboro Road.
23.8	Arrive at the Gallup Park parking lot.

RIDING WITH OTHER BICYCLISTS

Riding with other bicyclists can be a blast. You make new friends, learn about bicycling, go faster, and have the chance to socialize. Moreover, you can easily find people who ride like you do. Many group rides start together and rapidly self-segregate. Within a mile or so of the start the faster riders are long gone ahead of you, the slower ones have dropped behind, and you find yourself in a group of cyclists who ride exactly as fast as you want to ride.

The best way to learn to ride with a group is to do it with a bike club such as the AABTS. You'll quickly learn some of the key items of biking etiquette such as calling out notable objects (Car back! Dog up!) or noting the presence of obstacles such as branches and potholes in the road for riders following behind. Communication between bicyclists on the road can be essential for preventing accidents; far too many accidents are caused by unwanted bike-bike interactions.

Much of the effort in riding a bike is caused by the need to push yourself through the air. This wind resistence can be drastically reduced by riding closely behind another bicyclist, called "drafting." Drafting behind other bicyclists can be an exhilarating way to ride, but learn adequate bike-handling skills before you start and be sure to let the rider ahead know if you decide to draft behind.

"When the spirits are low, when the day appears dark, when work becomes monotonous, when hope seems hardly worth having, just mount a bicycle and go out for a good spin down the road, without thought of anything but the ride you are taking."

Arthur Conan Doyle, in *Scientific American* (1896)

℘ONTIAC TRAIL

ROUTE: Fuller Park, Ann Arbor, to corner of Pontiac Trail and Dixboro Road, 7.7 miles

LINKS WITH: Dixboro Road
Whitmore Lake Loop (via the Warren Road Option)

PARKING: Parking is available at Fuller Park, Ann Arbor.

This is a mainly uphill ride northeast out of Ann Arbor from residential to wooded areas with links to other options.

Turn right (west) out of Fuller Park and onto Fuller Road in the shadow of the University of Michigan Hospitals, which are straight ahead. Take care with the busy traffic in this area. Turn immediately right (northeast) on Maiden Lane (mile 0.2) to pass over the Huron River and continue straight past Broadway Street and Plymouth Road. Go through the traffic light (mile 0.7) as the road very briefly becomes Moore Street and turn sharply uphill to the right onto Pontiac Trail, riding up the first of many hills that you will confront in the early part of this ride.

You first go generally uphill through some older residential communities. Bike lanes appear and then disappear. As you approach an expressway (M-14) you will see Olson Park to your right (mile 2.4). This is one of Ann Arbor's newer parks, notable for a range of trails appropriate for mountain bikes. If you're on a cross bike or a mountain bike, it might be fun to check them out. (The park is marked as Dhu Varren Park on some older maps.) Shortly after crossing the expressway again at mile 2.7 the road continues to angle right, with Warren Road branching off to the left at mile 3.5.

- **OPTION:** Turn left on Warren Road and in only 1.0 miles you will come to Whitmore Lake Road and the Whitmore Lake Loop. ❖

As you ride northeast, Pontiac Trail angles through fields and parks, going mainly uphill. This road is an exception to the usual road orientation. Most roads in the county run either north-south or east-west; this road runs southwest-northeast.

At mile 7.2 you pass Northfield Park on the left, and at mile 7.7 you reach the intersection with Dixboro Road.

At Dixboro Road you have three options:

- Turn around, go back the way that you came, and enjoy the downhill ride!
- Turn right (south) on Dixboro Road and enjoy another downhill ride back into town! See the Dixboro Road route.
- Turn left (north) and extend your ride along Pontiac Trail with a loop into the South Lyon area. See the Dixboro Road route. ❖

ROUTE CUES:

0.0   Start at Fuller Park, Ann Arbor. Turn right (west) out of parking lot onto Fuller Road.

0.2   Turn right (northwest) onto Maiden Lane.

0.6   Proceed straight through the traffic light as the road becomes Moore Street.

0.7   Turn right (northeast) onto Pontiac Trail.

7.7   Arrive at the intersection of Pontiac Trail and Dixboro Road.

RIDING WITH A HELMET

Always ride with a helmet. Always. I know people who would likely be alive today were they wearing a helmet. Parents, please don't just insist that your children wear a helmet, wear one yourself. Helmets come in a wide range of styles and shapes, so anyone with any head size should be able to find one that is quite comfortable. They even come in bright colors, which can make you easy to spot in a group.

A helmet only works if it's on your head. Make sure it fits and is adjusted tightly enough to stay on in the event of a fall. If the helmet comes off, it's not going to do you any good. Nor is it going to do you any good if it's hanging from your handlebars!

No one goes out expecting to be in an accident. Yet accidents do happen. So wear a helmet every time you ride.

$\mathscr{G}$ALLUP PARK

ROUTE: Bike path through Gallup Park, 3 miles

LINKS WITH: Dixboro Road

PARKING: Parking is available at the eastern end of the park, off Dixboro Road, and at the main entrance, which is located just west of the intersection of Huron Parkway and Fuller Road. Bicycle riders who don't require parking can enter the park from the south by taking Devonshire Road and cutting through Devonshire Park, a nature area of 1.16 acres with a paved path running between residences at 2981 and 2989 Devonshire Road. This entrance requires riders to cross Geddes Road near a curve that blocks views of and from cars; adults with children will want to take special care.

This is a flat, traffic-free ride through one of Ann Arbor's loveliest parks.

Located along the Huron River in the city of Ann Arbor, Gallup Park is a sixty-nine-acre city park marked by arched bridges over a series of small islands and a pleasant, three-mile, paved path along the Huron River and Geddes Pond. The route runs along the river from the park's western terminus near the University of Michigan Hospitals to the eastern end near a dam on the Huron River. While bicyclists usually must share the path with walkers, Rollerbladers, and pets both large and small, the path offers a wonderful place to teach children to ride without having to deal with cars and too much fast-moving traffic. There are no hills to speak of, and, while the path crosses an entrance

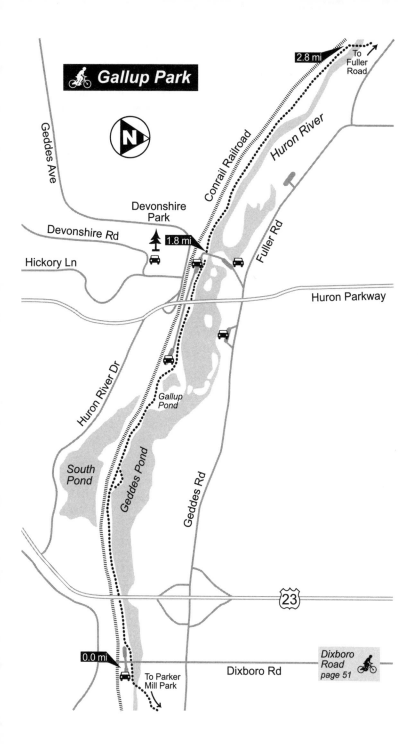

road, cars are moving slowly and the road should pose no hazard for supervised young riders.

The park offers much to do in addition to bicycle riding. It features playgrounds, picnic shelters, and (in season) a canoe livery that also rents paddleboats and kayaks. There is also a snack bar. Many types of wildlife are to be found along the path by the river or along a separate (nonbike) path through a wetland in the adjacent Furstenberg Park. The wildlife includes many, many Canada Geese, ducks, and their young ones at the appropriate time of year.

*"To sweep down hills and plunge into the valley hollows;
to cover as on wings the far stretches of the road ahead . . ."*
Alain-Fournier, *The Wanderer*

ℳANCHESTER

ROUTE: Loop from Pioneer High School, Ann Arbor, through
            Manchester, 49.6 miles

LINKS WITH: Dexter-Chelsea Road (via the Parker Road Option)
            Dexter-Chelsea Road (via Scio Church Road west to
            Highway M-52)

OPTIONS: Alternative start
            Parker Road Option
            West on Scio Church Road

PARKING: Parking is usually available at Pioneer High School,
            Ann Arbor, at the corner of Scio Church Road and
            Main Street.

*This ride passes through the scenic farm country of southern
Washtenaw County where the vistas are often a bit broader and the
ride less forested than in the northern parts of the county. About
halfway through, you visit the village of Manchester, which still
has some of the "feel" of a small town.*

The initial part of the ride goes along the seventeen-mile-long Scio
Church Road, named for a church located about halfway down the
road. This road can make for a pleasant ride if you schedule it when
cars are not too abundant. However, at times of heavy travel, the
growing number of housing developments in the area can lead to too
many cars on this narrow road for some bicyclists' comfort, especially
as the shoulder is slight to nonexistent. Moreover, the road is pretty
much straight for its entire length, which encourages drivers to go

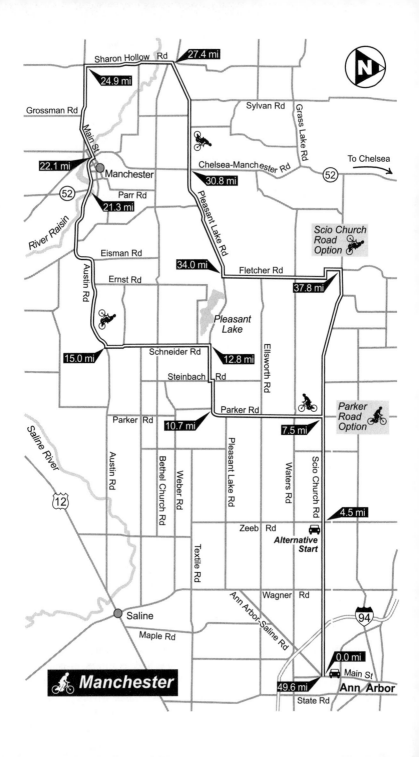

Colorful barn on Scio Church Road just west of Ann Arbor

faster than they might on a more winding path. So, unless you are very comfortable riding in traffic and sharing the road with cars, the portion of Scio Church Road east of Zeeb Road is best done on weekends or at other off-peak times.

Scio Church Road has its eastern terminus on Main Street in Ann Arbor, opposite the University of Michigan Golf Course and a short distance south of Michigan Stadium, the "Big House" where football Saturdays (best avoided for bicycling!) find over one hundred thousand fans gathered to cheer on the Maize and Blue. The start of the ride is just south of Pioneer High School, which has a huge parking lot.

Start at the corner of Scio Church Road and Main Street, heading west. The first few miles pass through residential parts of Ann Arbor, but you shortly ride over an expressway (I-94) and into more open countryside. You pass to your left facilities for indoor soccer, ice skating, hockey, and a host of other sports, and at mile 1.5 you pass a barn with a block M on the side. There are some gently rolling hills and fields interspersed with houses. At mile 4.5 you pass Emerson School on the left, cross Zeeb Road, and roll downhill into the rural environment that you will experience for the rest of the ride.

Egrets enjoying the wetland at the corner of Scio Church Road and Parker Road

ALTERNATIVE START. If you start the ride at the corner of Zeeb Road and Scio Church Road (Emerson School has a parking lot) you can avoid much of the in-town traffic. ❖

There are farms and fields on either side with a small cluster of houses around the church at mile 6.5. Note the brick house at 7570 Scio Church Road. It was completed in 1874 and is said to be one of the finest examples of Italianate architecture in the area. When you reach Parker Road at mile 7.5 stop for a few minutes on the gravel shoulder to experience the wetlands on either side of the road. They are delightfully different as the seasons change with varying amounts of plants, water (or ice), and a plethora of wildlife, especially birds. In the spring the frogs may be making a racket; in the fall you can watch birds coming in for a rest on their way to warmer climes. I've seen egrets, nesting swans, ducks, geese, and a fair number of other birds I've not been able to identify.

You can go in any direction from the intersection of Parker and Scio Church for pleasant riding. The main route, detailed here, will take you on a loop to Manchester. If you don't want to go that far you can turn around and go back the way you came. Or you can take one of two other options.

- **OPTIONAL ROUTE NORTH ON PARKER ROAD TO DEXTER-CHELSEA ROAD,** 5.6 miles. This is a reasonably straight and flat ride that will take you over the expressway (I-94) and past Dexter High School to the intersection of Parker Road and Dexter-Chelsea Road, which links to the Dexter-Chelsea route. From there you can go east and into Dexter (and link to several routes) or west and into Chelsea (and also link to several routes).

- **OPTIONAL ROUTE WEST ON SCIO CHURCH ROAD TO HIGHWAY M-52,** 7.1 miles. If you continue straight on Scio Church Road, going due west, you will have a very nice, seven-mile stretch of rolling hills, fields, and occasional glimpses of water. There are some dirt roads branching off on either side, and if you are on a suitable bike they make for a nice network of country rides. After about 4 miles you reach Fletcher Road on your left, which is where the main loop to Manchester rejoins Scio Church Road on the way back to Ann Arbor. You can get to Manchester from here by reversing the loop; the ride is very pleasant in both directions.

  If you go straight on Scio Church Road after its intersection with Fletcher Road, in about 3 miles you will reach highway M-52. This is a busy road, although it has a generous shoulder in most places. You can go north for three miles into Chelsea and take one of the routes through that city. The highway also goes south to Manchester, but if you want to ride to Manchester there are better ways to go. Or you can turn around and go back the way that you came. ❖

For the main ride to Manchester, turn south from Scio Church onto Parker Road. The road will naturally turn to the right (west) at mile 10.7; while Parker Road continues south as a dirt road you will follow the paved road around as it becomes Pleasant Lake Road, which was apparently named for a pleasant lake a few miles down the road. You'll be turning off before you reach the lake on this ride to Manchester. Stay on Pleasant Lake Road as it makes a short turn to the south and then straightens out headed west. You'll be passing a few farms and can enjoy the sights, sounds, and smells of the area. Then turn south on Schneider Road at mile 12.8.

This road will take you up and down some of the best hills in Washtenaw County and up to Bethel Church and its cemetery. Catch your breath, take a drink of water, and admire the beautiful views! Continue south, picking up speed on the well-earned downhill to a dead end at Austin Road at mile 15.0. Turn right (west) on Austin Road as it winds its way through fields and farms and meets up with M-52 at mile 21.3. Go straight on M-52 heading into Manchester, home of a world-famous fund-raising chicken broil held each summer at which over ten thousand chicken dinners are served in just a few hours. The road crosses the River Raisin, named for the clusters of wild grapes that once graced its shores. This river was at one time a major transportation route that allowed travel from Lake Erie to Lake Michigan with only a short portage.

Continue past the fairgrounds to Main Street. Turn left (west) to go into the center of town at mile 22.1. You are now near the halfway point on this ride. Manchester makes for a nice stopping point if you are so inclined. There is a pleasant bakery on your right with some tables outside. On busy weekend mornings you might get to share one of the large tables inside. Or stop in at the Whistle Stop Café, a popular breakfast spot. If you have brought a snack with you it can be enjoyed down the road at Carr Park on your left.

Once you are suitably refueled and watered, continue west out of town on Main Street, which becomes Austin Road, and turn right (north) on Sharon Hollow Road at mile 24.9. Note the barn just past

Cows reflected in the pond on Pleasant Lake Road

Sharon Mills County Park, once the site of a Ford factory, outside of Manchester

the turn on your left, at 16991 Austin Road, which has an interesting and unusual shape. It's replicated in red down the road at 7523 Sharon Hollow Road. As you continue north on Sharon Hollow Road, take a slight jog to the left and then the right to stay on the main road. At the bottom of the hill you again come to the River Raisin, this time at the site of an attractive park with an interesting history.

The River Raisin, like many southeastern Michigan rivers, long served as an important source of power. Starting in the 1850s a gristmill stood at this site. Near the end of the nineteenth century, steam power became widespread and many mills ceased operation (see the Huron River Drive route). Rather than becoming yet another abandoned mill, this structure on the river became part of the burgeoning automobile industry as one of Henry Ford's broad-minded innovations.

Rather than concentrating automobile manufacturing in one place, Ford thought that he should distribute some of the work in the countryside. This idea of "village industry" was based on the notion of having "one foot in industry and one in the soil," a contrast with the usual urban-based assembly lines and factories of the (then) thriving automobile industry. In 1939 Ford converted the mill on the River Raisin

An interesting barn on Fletcher Road

to a hydroelectric plant and utilized the energy to make cigar lighters for Ford vehicles. After he abandoned the site in 1946 it was used as a private residence and then a winery. It is now Sharon Mills Country Park, a very attractive park used for weddings and celebrations and a nice place to stop and stretch your legs, especially if you passed up the chance to stop in Manchester.

Turning right (north) out of the parking lot you continue on Sharon Hollow Road on a hill that feels a lot tougher than it first appears. The paved road curves to the right (east) and becomes Pleasant Lake Road again at mile 27.4. Note the centennial farms in the area, farms that have been in the same family for over one hundred years.

On the north side of the road at the intersection with M-52, at mile 30.8, sits the gothic revival Salem United Methodist Church, established in 1874 to serve the German Methodist community of the area. One of its cemeteries was for early settlers from the northeastern United States; the other was mainly for the ethnic Germans who made up a large settlement from the 1830s until the Second World War. Many of the farms seen in this area were originally settled by immigrants from Germany, and services in the local churches were held exclusively in German until well into the twentieth century.

On the northeast corner of the M-52/Pleasant Lake Road intersection is a grass landing strip, from which in good weather you can see gliders being towed aloft. On the southwest corner is a convenience store.

Going straight on Pleasant Lake Road, after some impressive scenic vistas, turn left (north) on Fletcher Road at mile 34.0. At 4354 Fletcher Road note the interesting nineteenth-century barn with its main entrance located on the gable rather than along the elevated side.

You also pass the Zion Lutheran Church, built in 1867 in the gothic revival style. The road jogs left and then right and then comes to Scio Church Road at mile 37.8.

- **OPTIONAL ROUTE WEST.** At this point, you can turn left (west) and ride to M-52 and perhaps to Chelsea. ❖

Turn right (east) on Scio Church Road and retrace your path to Ann Arbor, crossing Parker Road at mile 42.1 and returning to your starting point at mile 49.6.

ROUTE CUES:

0.0	Start at the corner of Scio Church Road and Main Street, Ann Arbor. Go west on Scio Church Road.
1.4	Pass over I-94.
4.5	Cross Zeeb Road. Note Emerson School on the left, the alternative start.
7.5	Turn left (south) onto Parker Road.
10.7	Turn right (west) as the main road becomes Pleasant Lake Road.
12.8	Turn left (south) onto Schneider Road.
15.9	Turn right (east) onto Austin Road.
21.0	Continue into Manchester as Austin Road joins M-52 and then crosses the River Raisin.
21.3	Continue on M-52.
22.1	Turn left (west) on Main Street, which becomes Austin Road as you leave town.
24.9	Turn right (north) on Sharon Hollow Road.
26.5	Jog to left and then right on Sharon Hollow Road.
27.1	Pass Sharon Mills County Park.
27.4	Veer right on the paved road as Sharon Hollow Road becomes Pleasant Lake Road.
30.8	Cross M-52.

34.0   Turn left (north) on Fletcher Road.

37.0   Jog to the left and then right on Fletcher Road.

37.8   Turn right (east) on Scio Church Road.

42.1   Cross Parker Road.

45.1   Cross Zeeb Road. Emerson School is on the right.

49.6   Arrive at the corner of Scio Church Road and Main Street
        in Ann Arbor.

RIDING FOR HEALTH

There's no doubt that riding on the road exposes you to an element of risk. You can go fast, but cars are big (and can go faster). Bicycling is inherently dangerous. However, it is an excellent form of lifetime exercise, and the health benefits of exercise for almost everyone are becoming ever more clear. You are far more likely to continue an exercise routine if you love what you are doing. Many people love to ride a bicycle, and riding can be a lifelong way to stay active. If you suffer from a chronic disease, however, you should check with your physician before starting any new exercise program.

RIDING AND EATING

Bike riding is a great way to burn calories. You can be out for a long time having a great time. But for any sort of long ride you need to eat and drink. Water is always important. If you are going any sort of distance, take some food as well. There are a wide range of energy bars to choose from along with concentrated "goo," a dense, compact calorie source found at bicycle shops. I personally find bananas and M&Ms washed down with lukewarm water hard to beat!

Listen to your body. If you feel thirsty, drink (and drink even if you don't feel thirsty). If you feel hungry, eat. If you don't, you run the risk of "bonking," a sense that your energy level has dropped almost to zero. It's not a pleasant feeling.

AREA BIKE SHOPS

Recommended local bike shops include:

ABERDEEN BIKE AND FITNESS
1178 South Main, Chelsea
734.475.8203

ANN ARBOR CYCLERY
1200 Packard, Ann Arbor
734.761.2749

DEXTER BIKE AND SPORT
3173 Baker Road, Dexter
734.426.5900

GREAT LAKES CYCLING AND FITNESS
2107 West Stadium, Ann Arbor
734.668.6484

RIDE BOUTIQUE
924 North Main, Ann Arbor
734.662.0544

TWO WHEEL TANGO
3162 Packard, Ann Arbor
734.528.3030

and

4765 Jackson Road, Ann Arbor
734.769.8401

WHEELS IN MOTION CYCLE AND FITNESS
3400 Washtenaw, Ann Arbor
734.971.2121

BIBLIOGRAPHY

BIKE ROUTES

These books can provide an introduction to other bicycle riding options in Michigan. Some of these titles, alas, appear no longer to be in print.

Gentry, Karen. *30 of the Best Bike Routes in East Michigan.* Grand Rapids: Thunder Bay Press, 1995.

Noga, Cari. *Road Biking Michigan.* Guilford, CT: Globe Pequot Press, 2005.

Stovall, Pamela. *Short Bike Rides in Michigan.* 2nd ed. Guilford, CT: Globe Pequot Press, 1998.

Van Valkenberg, Phil. *The Best Bike Rides in the Midwest.* Old Saybrook, CT: Globe Pequot Press, 1994.

BICYCLING BOOKS

There is no shortage of bicycling books. These are some of my favorites.

Cuthbertson, Tom. *Anybody's Bike Book: An Original Manual of Bicycle Repairs.* Berkeley, CA: Ten Speed Press, 1990. A wonderfully idiosyncratic and entertaining yet very practical guide.

Forester, John. *Effective Cycling,* 6th ed. Cambridge: MIT Press, 1993. Lots of very useful advice for safe bicycling.

Hurst, Robert. *The Art of Cycling: A Guide to Bicycling in Twenty-first-Century America.* Guilford, CT: Globe Pequot Press, 2007. Mainly about urban bicycling with lots of good tips.

Mionske, Bob. *Bicycling and the Law: Your Rights as a Cyclist.* Boulder: Velo Press, 2007. You have rights, but you have responsibilities as well.

Starrs, James E. ed. *The Noiseless Tenor: The Bicycle in Literature.* New York: Cornwall Books, 1982. A delightful collection of readings.

Strickland, Bill, ed. *The Quotable Cyclist: Great Moments of Bicycling Wisdom, Inspiration, and Humor.* Halcottsville, NY: Breakaway Books, 2001. Topical quotations on a wide range of bicycling subjects.

Tracy, Sam. *Bicycle! A Repair and Maintenance Manifesto.* Denver: Speck Press, 2006. Bicycle repair with attitude.

Wilson, David Gordon. *Bicycling Science.* 3rd ed. Cambridge: MIT Press, 2004. Everything you ever wanted to know about the fundamentals of this human-powered vehicle.

Zinn, Lennard. *Zinn and the Art of Road Bike Maintenance.* Boulder: Velo Press, 2000. Excellent illustrations and clear explanations.

ABOUT THE AUTHOR

JOEL HOWELL is an avid cyclist who has been obsessed with bicycle riding in and around Ann Arbor for the past fifteen years. While he has occasionally debated whether to start on a bike ride, once he has gone out on a ride he has never been sorry that he did. When not riding a bicycle, he is the Victor Vaughan Professor of the History of Medicine at the University of Michigan, where he is a professor of internal medicine, history, and health management and policy.

RIDING LOG

DATE	TIME	ROUTE	DISTANCE	WEATHER	CLOTHING	SPEED	COMMENTS

DATE	TIME	ROUTE	DISTANCE	WEATHER	CLOTHING	SPEED	COMMENTS

RIDING LOG

DATE	TIME	ROUTE	DISTANCE	WEATHER	CLOTHING	SPEED	COMMENTS

DATE	TIME	ROUTE	DISTANCE	WEATHER	CLOTHING	SPEED	COMMENTS

RIDING LOG

DATE	TIME	ROUTE	DISTANCE	WEATHER	CLOTHING	SPEED	COMMENTS

DATE	TIME	ROUTE	DISTANCE	WEATHER	CLOTHING	SPEED	COMMENTS

Text design and composition by Jillian Downey
Text font: Janson
Display font: Today SB

Although designed by the Hungarian Nicholas Kis in about 1690, the model for Janson Text was mistakenly attributed to the Dutch printer Anton Janson. Kis' original matrices were found in Germany and acquired by the Stempel foundry in 1919. This version of Janson comes from the Stempel foundry and was designed from the original type; it was issued by Linotype in digital form in 1985.

—courtesy www.adobe.com

Today SB was designed by Volker Küster in 2004 and is owned by Scangraphic PrePress Technology GmbH.

—courtesy www.myfonts.com